PANORAMAS OF ENGLAND

PANORAMAS OF ENGLAND
Text by Adam Nicolson · Photographs by Nick Meers

PREVIOUS PAGE

Dunstanburgh Castle,
Northumberland

OVERLEAF

Blea Tarn, Cumbria

SWALEDALE, NEAR THWAITE, NORTH YORKSHIRE

PREVIOUS PAGE
*New River Bridge and
Hawksmoor's Mauso-
leum, Castle Howard,
North Yorkshire*

THE LONG MAN OF WILMINGTON, EAST SUSSEX

INTRODUCTION

Puffins marry their burrows. Or at least they do for the four or five weeks every year they spend on land. For the rest of their lives they float about, quite alone, on the waters of the North Atlantic. But every spring the puffins return to the colony that bred them. For a few days they do not actu- ally fly up on to the land. Instead, in huge, squawking rafts, they hold a party on the sea, having for this brief, libertarian moment in an otherwise rather straitened existence an utterly promiscuous time, flirting with and seducing an almost endless succession of partners. There is no establishment of steady mates, no sign of loyalty or love. The bays and channels off the coast of the colony provide for a day or two the most generous of water beds.

Then the great change: the puffins go ashore, flying up on to the grassy slopes that are pockmarked with their burrows. They always return to the burrow they occupied the previous year, and so of course the previous year's couples, which hadn't featured in the puffin imagination while out at sea – no puffin can, apparently, tell the difference between other puffins – find themselves reassembling. In this way puffin marriages remain constant for life, not because they are loyal to each other but because they are both loyal to their place, to that little, rather dirty hole dug a couple of feet into the hillside. Every puffin, in fact, marries a tiny bit of landscape which another puffin happens to have married too. And so they breed.

Home is the great bond of puffin society. When the need for home disappears and the chick is successfully bred and fed, the puffins disperse, forget each other and their children, and think of nothing but their winter-long isolation adrift on the ocean until the moment comes the following year when the need for home reintroduces them to their wives.

It occurs to me that the beautiful and captivating photographs in this book are something like our burrow. They are the places that unite us. Almost without exception, they are pictures of the supremely known, the elements of a version of England which, if we were incarcerated in a dank, hostile, foreign gaol, might float up in our daydreams as images not exactly of release and freedom but of return and reacceptance into the things with which we felt at home. They are pictures of the places to which the English are married.

The right word is 'we'. This is the landscape of the first person plural. They are not, on the whole, depictions of the Wordsworthian sublime or Byronic isolation – nothing as brave or extreme as that, not Romantic in that sense – but of a deeply shared, and perhaps deeply needed, sense of comfort. The landscape which together these pictures create in the mind – and of course we know as we look at them they are not true to the real state of the country, that they are the most obvious of selective fictions – is really nothing more than the national sofa: old, familiar, receptive, rounded and, above all, ours.

THE HOPE VALLEY, DERBYSHIRE

SEVEN SISTERS FROM BIRLING GAP, EAST SUSSEX

unsupervision there (look at the bluebells at Littledean on pages 84–5); the floating of boats in streams and the flooding of small channels; collecting chestnuts, burning marshmallows in the fire; the first all-day bicycle rides; that sudden fresh-air teenage sensation (I remember it on a winter weekend in a gale in Derbyshire) that the landscape is something you can move endlessly through, the connectedness of all places; then those rather threatening, hot, pre-sexual afternoons and, later, the after-party middles-of-the-night. (I will always see Leicestershire in a way I imagine no-one else will share because when I lived there I had a car with no roof and used to drive on moonlit nights with the headlights off and the hunting country as blue around me as a room lit by nothing but the pale electric light of a television screen.)

So, in a personal and private way, England thickens around you, becomes a reservoir of personal meanings, a succession of reminders as you move through it again of what you have been and what you have done. But at the same time something else is going on, a parallel accumulation of meanings as you come to know that what you think about England is usually no more than the reflection and refraction of what people have thought and written before. England is crowded with the Great. There is no wilderness there. In every one of the landscapes photographed in this book there is a mass of men and women standing shoulder to shoulder, jostling for room on the hillside or the

This padded, lie-back country belongs to us in a sense which, almost uniquely in a nation so divided by the signals of class and status, *crosses* those half-hidden and subtle boundaries. These are the places where everybody, no matter what class or background they come from, wants to own a cottage or go for a walk, which everybody considers – in a word so degraded that it is now almost unusable – lovely, lovable and representing the sort of feeling, presumably, that a puffin might have as he sees his burrow again, a recognition of belonging.

So what is this England to which the prisoner finds himself so longingly attached? It is a big, baggy and amorphous thing, all-dimensional, wide in space and deep in time and bound up for everybody with elements of their own autobiography: the first expedition to the wood on your own, the magical

CHATSWORTH, DERBYSHIRE

lawn, who have seen this, made this, venerated this, enshrined this before. Sometimes the records and memories of their lives and work seem to rustle around you like a field of standing wheat. But often it is noisier than that, a chattering, crowded party room, filled with the remarks of the dead, where the gabbling of old friends, the meaningful silence of the melancholic in the corner by the drinks, the sharpness and gossip of the wits and urbanites, the excluded men, the men of the moment, where all this pushes in. What you think you think is no more than the babble of their conversation, the noise of a party heard on the lawn outside.

But who are they, these shared authors of a fictional England? Who has created these landscapes of the utterly familiar? No one, I think, from before the Renaissance continues to have an effect on the way we think of this picture-England. The whole way in which people looked at their surroundings shifted in the sixteenth century so that the medieval vision of nature, its detailed attention to the columbine and the cony, honeysuckle on the hedges, jewelled daisies underfoot, gave way to something both larger and more removed. The idea of landscape itself appears towards the end of the sixteenth century as the twin of a new kind of independent, self-sufficient man. He is removed from nature, it is removed from him and as a result nature or the landscape gains a coherence it did not have before. The medieval type is, say, the Chaucerian pilgrim scarcely noticing or engaging with the surroundings of the road to Canterbury except in terms of the seasons or the flowering or the fruiting of the plants at his side. The landscape — and that is not an idea or a word that emerges before about 1600 — is so close to him that he doesn't see it as a thing. In medieval pictures the landscape, where it even appears, is a background, as shallow as wallpaper and spotted with the minutiae of the natural world, as if the whole of nature were organized as simply – and chaotically – as the pimpling of crocuses on an orchard floor.

The Renaissance type, by contrast, is perhaps King Lear. He could not be more distinct from the hostile, difficult and alien heath on which he finds himself in his crisis. The landscape has taken on for him a terrifying and – more important – a coherent reality. It has become a thing in itself.

Lear is a figure set in a world where there is a true sense of perspective. It is no coincidence that this new vision of the landscape as something else, as an object, emerges at the same time as the idea of nationhood, of England itself. The first real maps of the country, John of Gaunt's 'this realm' speech in *Richard II*, the first real Histories of England, the first perspective views of country houses and their estates, the first time, in the famous 'Ditchley' portrait of Queen Elizabeth, that a monarch is shown standing as a giant on the map of the country, the first time that great houses come to be set in an aesthetic, designed way in the landscape – all these represent a new way of looking at the world in which place, nation and landscape all become deeply connected. The pictorial sense of the landscape comes now to embody the soul of the nation. The idea of 'Panoramas of England' was born in our late, northern Renaissance.

But Lear is an unsatisfactory or at least a primitive ancestor. He is not like us; he's too difficult, too agonized. We are now a great deal cosier with the landscape of England and few of us go into paroxysms of self-knowledge on the heath outside Bournemouth. But Lear is at least a distant relative in the

FIELD OF RAPE, NEAR KINETON, GLOUCESTERSHIRE

sense that the medieval continuity between the person and the place has been broken in him. He embodies the loss of innocence. As a tragic figure, he finds the gap between him and his landscape almost unbearable. But for most of the English that gap which opened up between man and nature has fuelled a gentler and sweeter version of alienation: pastoral. The pastoral idea – that happiness can be found again by returning to the nature you have left behind – has been the major force in shaping and moulding the vision of

advertisements and National Trust appeal leaflets, in the buying of woolly jerseys and corduroy trousers. Pastoral is perhaps the English disease.

It is of course a delusion, but the fact of a shared delusion has itself been the governing and shaping reality. Milton, in *Paradise Lost*, can sound at times, when describing Paradise itself, like an estate agent recommending the beauties of a great aristocratic landscape of the following century:

> *Thus was this place,*
> *A happy rural seat of various view . . .*
> *Betwixt them lawns, or level downs, and flocks*
> *Grazing the tender herb were interposed,*
> *Or palmy hillock, or the flowery lap*
> *Of some irriguous valley spread her store,*
> *Flowers of all hue, and without thorn the rose.*
> *Another side, umbrageous grots and caves*
> *Of cool recess, o'er which the mantling vine*
> *Lays forth her purple grape, and gently creeps*
> *Luxuriant; meanwhile murmuring waters fall*
> *Down the slope hills, dispersed, or in a lake,*
> *That to a fringèd bank with myrtle crowned*
> *Her crystal mirror holds, unite their streams.*

picture-England in the last 400 years. Pastoral describes the home – the notional burrow – which we are destined never to find because, by definition, it can never be the place where we find ourselves. Its modern form is not in drama or poetry, where for centuries it flowered happily enough, but in photographs. This book is an exercise in pastoral, England dressed in the dream coating of perfect, dawn-lit colour photography, but it appears elsewhere all the time: in the property pages of *Country Life*, in car

Thousands of acres of eighteenth-century England were radically and expensively reshaped according to this pattern. Its creamy, continuous, smart and perfected version of the temperate landscape (look at Bowood or Holkham) remains today one vision of how the country needs to be. Nothing is

PEVENSEY CASTLE, EAST SUSSEX

disruptive in the 'happy rural seat of various view'. Everything is gentle, everything murmurs. It is the grand unruffled scene, ordered according to the loosened, understated rules of decorum which govern the behaviour of the supremely privileged. The park at Holkham looks the way Adam would have behaved in Paradise. Or – more visually – its attitudes and langour are those of the Adam who lounges so beautifully muscled on the ceiling of the Sistine Chapel. All human capabilities are there, but what does Adam do? He slowly dangles a single finger out towards his God.

But there is another picture, closer to home, in which this England comes to a point, to a distillation of comfort and a certain kind of content. James Thomson, the great country-house poet of the first half of the eighteenth century, was a fat man. 'A bard here dwelt,' he once quite charmingly wrote of himself, 'more fat than bard beseems'. He was spotted one summer afternoon (he never got up before lunch) standing in his garden, hands in pockets, eating the sunny side off the peaches still hanging from the espaliered trees. He then wandered inside to extol the perfected beauties of yet another perfectly arranged estate.

This nibbling of the over-comfortable man marks the very end of a certain development. Something had to give and all the radical discontents, the sudden passions and bursting metaphysical disquiet of the Romantics come thundering in behind that vision of James Thomson's lips and teeth. When John Clare wrote about the little moles, the mouldiwarps, strung up by the landlord's men on what used to be common ground, his rage and regret is the product of his own vision of England, the gentle, detailed and unpowerful, banging up against another, the powerful, imposing, comfortable and grand,

O I never call to mind
Those pleasant names of places but I leave a sigh behind
While I see the little mouldiwarps hang sweeing to the wind
On the only aged willow that in all the field remains
And nature hides her face while theyre sweeing in their chains
And in a silent murmuring complains.

Reading Clare, a sudden understanding grips you of what the imposition of a proprietor's Eden involved, of seeing England as a view and ignoring the small and local things. The mouldiwarps stand for the villagers displaced because they cluttered a view, the poachers caught in the man-traps, the real peasants watching the pantomime pastoral which was meant to represent their delighted lives. It is a sudden searching light cast on the self-delusion and wish-fulfilment of pastoral.

A cousin feeling of distaste emerges in Keats, in his contempt for all the fakeries of Travel Writing, as practised then and now: 'I put down,' he wrote in a letter to a friend, 'Mountains, Rivers, lakes, dells, glens, Rocks, and Clouds, With beautiful, enchanting, gothic picturesque fine, delightful, enchancting, Grand, sublime – a few Blisters & c – and now you have our journey thus far . . .'; for the dreadful blindness to reality in literary tourism: 'O the flummery of a birth place! Cant! Cant! Cant! It is enough to give a spirit the guts ache . . . I cannot write about scenery and visitings.' What matters to Clare and Keats is not the pastoral, the smoothed view and its associations but the more specific reality. As Keats later wrote to his brother, 'Nothing ever becomes real till it is experienced.'

This, in modern form, is perhaps a return to the medieval vision, to the anti-systematic view of the world, in which large, complete scenic effects fall apart into the details of which they are made. And where large scenic effects are achieved at the expense of a real intimacy with the world of real things, as inevitably they must be, then the large effect is a fake and a lie. In this new Romantic attitude, perhaps, the origins of an ecological understanding of landscape itself – rather than the imposed pastoral vision – can be found.

It is not as if a new attitude replaces an old. We all, in our different ways, continue to nibble the hanging peach, but the coming of Romanticism adds something else to the understanding of the landscape. The partial, the incomplete, the glimpsed fragment, the tatty and the unsmoothed all become symbolic of something valuable which cannot be approached by the smooth aesthetics of an earlier view. The vision of detail takes its place alongside the wide, panoramic spread, the estate owner's survey.

But I wonder if one can make out today which parts of this layered inheritance we choose to shape our idea of England, or at least of this picture-England, the national sofa? Where does our comfort lie, with Milton and Thomson or with Keats and Clare? Both visions of the country are nowadays embraced by the idea of 'conservation', but that is a term which is tending towards the state of 'democracy': everybody loves it and everybody means different things by it. The National Trust, the conservation body with two million members, managed, for example, to plough up an entire medieval field system at Wimpole Hall in Cambridgeshire. It was done in the name of tidiness and the improvement of a grand eighteenth-century landscape. In Wasdale Head the Trust, as landlords, pay for the repair of stone walls that are next to the road but not those further in and which are unseen from cars. Appearance is all for James Thomson England, now as it always has been.

But the Clare–Keats way of seeing things has begun to take hold. The big view is beginning to be seen as not enough. The Trust now conducts detailed biological surveys on its properties. There is perhaps a growing dissatisfaction with visual perfection. Or at least the idea of perfection may not now be quite as tidy as it was. People want a little raggedness, for the sort of near-formlessness you might find in Wistman's Wood on Dartmoor or the unpatterned muddle of a Cornish hedge in spring.

Over a century ago William Morris appealed for the principle of 'anti-scrape' in the restoration of ancient buildings, for a casual, dangling ordinariness in the look of a place, not the pat, delivered, swept, drawing-room style. But even 'anti-scrape' is too programmatic as a principle. Some places need sweeping and Swaledale would be diminished if it did not have an annual haytime laundering. But the ragged edge of a Cumbrian tarn, the scruff of growth in marshland ditches, the imprecision of Wicken Fen – the actual value, or even the apparent, visual quality, resides in this failure to tidy. To preserve what is valuable in the look of a place it is important that it should not appear as if its essential nature has been falsified. Keep the Somerset Levels crudely shorn, whatever the underlying realities might be of control, bureaucratization or government subsidy of an environmentally sensitive area. Keep the park at Holkham smooth. That is what the English want these places to be.

The time has certainly passed when the ultimate priority in the English countryside was agricultural production. It has become, for the most part, an

HALZEPHRON CLIFF, THE LIZARD, CORNWALL

aesthetic pleasure-zone, the pleasure grounds of a city-dwelling nation, the place to be visited not worked in. It is the garden not the allotment of the nation. And like a garden the overriding concern is the look of the place. That does not mean that neatness and completeness is the only face it should show. As even sixteenth-century gardeners knew, there is a place for wildness (or relative wildness, anyway) as a counterpart to order and control. It can be a garden of which both Thomson and Clare would have approved.

Once you can think of the whole English landscape in this way, there is no difficulty in accepting that our attitudes towards it are not 'real'; that farmers should be paid to do pretty not productive things; that people want to keep some places quite astonishingly neat and clean. I know one village in the Cotswolds where the residents have forced a local farmer to hose down the village street after driving through it in his muddy tractor; and another, Chipping Campden, where housing is now so expensive that a local farmer has to bus in his – predominantly Sikh – labour from Birmingham every day. In many ways England has already become indistinguishable from 'England'.

But is that enough? Isn't it something of a disappointment to think of this country as such a delicately and effectively *managed* place, with its little flick of wildness here and there, with its *bien soigné* washed coiffure, where climax is slight and the sense of grandeur minuscule, where drama is prosaic and life itself now rather muted, and where, most debilitatingly of all, the sense of its own history is so dominant that 'steeped in history' – a formaldehyde phrase – becomes the District Council's relished description of any half-likely, tourist-generating honeypot? Historic Maidstone? Is there nothing more than that? Has everything been done already?

George Herbert, the seventeenth-century mystic and poet, once described the landscape of England, in a phrase designed to tease the over-rigid sensibilities of the Puritans, as 'the back-parts of the Deity'. It is an unforgettable and wonderful description, a delighted, laughing recognition of all the connections between heaven and earth, between particular fields, woods and streams and something universal. It is the understanding that the surface on which we all find ourselves is nothing more – nor less – than God's bottom. Three hundred years later, that sort of idea, the idea that the landscape of England is in some oblique way sacred, is virtually absent, except perhaps in the cranky and ill-founded schemes of ley-liners and those who can trace the outlines of the Zodiac in the fields and hedges around Glastonbury. But it is too good an idea to be left to the cranks. Ronald Blythe has called this abandoned sense of the sacred landscape 'the complex underlying holy land' of England. It is more visible – or at least the habit of mind that recognizes it is more visible – abroad. In the Himalayas every ridge is given its cluster of poles on which the prayer flags can blow; every stream a small water-wheel and mill designed to turn not a pair of millstones but a prayer wheel which, in its turning, makes explicit the holiness of the stream running through it. 'Thy pasture is thy word: the streams thy grace,' Herbert wrote, with the directness and clarity that marks him out as a kind of saint. Do we have sacred streams in England any more? Probably not. The stream by which William Langland lay down to sleep and dream of Piers Plowman now runs straight into the Schweppes Malvern Water factory; it emerges in bottles.

This claim to sanctity does not have anything to do with druids in their dressing gowns and sheets, nor with the established church which either

avoids the issue or banalizes it. The landscape of England is sacred only in the sense that almost anyone can recognize who has been moved by a place, (this in the end is an attitude that comes from Wordsworth): the ineffable sensation of something there beyond the material facts.

To be any more explicit is not a fashionable or in the end very sayable thing. The vocabulary has fallen away. When George Orwell edged an inch or two beyond the secular orthodoxy and wrote in his *Tribune* columns about the pleasure of seeing his Woolworth's roses grow, or of the peculiar radiance in the eye of the common toad, or the coming of spring and the sight of the swallows dipping in and out of the gasometer girders in north London, his post filled with complaints about irrelevance and sentimentality. Of course, he responded with the vigour and humane reasonableness you would expect. But there have been those this century who, without being cranky and recognizing the difficulty of seeing the landscape like this, have dared to go much further. There was W. H. Auden's sudden recognition on a summer evening in the 1930s of a wonderful and almost unrepeated moment when

> *Fear gave his watch no look;*
> *The lion griefs loped from the shade*
> *And on our knees their muzzles laid*
> *And Death put down his book.*

It was a moment not a place, or at least a moment of perfection hinged to a particular place. And that, I think, is what the peculiarly English sense of pastoral remains. These photographs are of places where a kind of perfection *might* happen.

But the English are not good at remembering that. All too easily they remember a happy time and turn it into a happy place. And the whole history of attitudes to rural England in the last hundred years makes it clear that the nation does feel that particular parts of the country are somehow life-enhancing in themselves. Lower Slaughter and the Seven Sisters, Upper Wasdale and the Wylye valley, these are the expensive, the truly valued spots. The needs that drive, for example, the growth of the National Trust, the creation of National Parks, Areas of Outstanding Natural Beauty, the Countryside Commission National Trails and so on are all focused on the idea of the perfectly happy place. And that idea now plays the part of a very soft form of the national religion, a religion whose foundation is pure comfort. The English countryside is now the English God.

So dream time in picture-England becomes an escape into the undemandingly familiar, to places which you can consider yours in some vague and undefined way, and where you have rights but no responsibilities, a limited sort of freedom and no anxiety. It is for this reason that people almost never appear in picture-England. People make demands and will not always cooperate. People are difficult; picture-England never can be. This is a change in the last fifty years or so. 'Country characters' – the stand by of *Picture Post* articles, or country writing before the war – rarely feature nowadays. Photographed England now looks as if a neutron bomb has hit it: no damage to buildings or landscapes but people have been utterly removed.

Of course, the cumulative landscape that you will find in this book is, in many ways, an empty vessel. Halzephron Cliff on the Lizard might just as well be in Brittany or the Cotentin. Hope Valley in Derbyshire might, at a stretch, be part of northern California; Chatsworth, perhaps, a rather unknown schloss outside Wiesbaden. But they are not and everything the English continue to think about England is poured into these pictures like milk into a bucket. They seem to be overbrimming with the English national consciousness, which is not consciousness of a flag, or a language or even really a race, but of a landscape. The National Front never really had a chance in England but if the National Trust stood as a political party, particularly at a time of recession or crisis, it would be interesting to see how it performed.

So these pictures, which meander clockwise and a little haphazardly around the country, beginning in the south-east, going west and then north before returning to London, represent the shared vision of place, the root meaning of England, the sort of associations a puffin might have with his burrow.

OXBURGH HALL, NORFOLK

THE PANORAMAS

BEACHY HEAD
East Sussex

If you tipped the Royal Crescent at Bath on its end, it would just fit between the turf on top of Beachy Head and the sea below. The cliff is England's most dramatic beginning. All the subtle modulations of the South Downs come rolling along, nothing suspected, to this sudden lip. And there, as if with a cheese-wire, the sea slices straight through the lot. It is the sort of place where you must approach on hands and knees, edging up to the crumbly edge, for the instant, stomach-dropping view down into the substance of England, through the fifteen million years of accumulation that this chalk cliff represents, pin-striped with its layers of flint, to the Victorian lighthouse below. Richard Jefferies haunts this place. 'The glory of these glorious Downs', he wrote 'is the breeze. It is the air without admixture. If it comes from the south the waves refine it; if inland the wheat and flowers and grass distil it. The great headland and the whole rib of the promontory is windswept and washed with air; the billows of the atmosphere roll over it.'

WEST FIRLE
East Sussex

The lower limbs of a Sussex Down, now covered in a cornfield, drop to the woods and heavier clays of the Weald, which stretches to the skyline, about six hours walk away, and on again as far beyond that to the matching chalk of the North Downs in Kent. The village of West Firle is gathered around the spring that emerges where the chalk meets the clay. The parish, as in all these Down-foot villages, runs in a long strip north and south of the church – out on one side into the woodland and hedged fields of the Weald, and, on the other, up onto the sheep-walks of the Downs to the south. It is the margin between two worlds. Until this century it was a definite boundary between the pastoral and the agricultural, between the double resource of a corn and sheep village, a pattern of use hinged to the underlying nature of the rocks. That distinction has now been smoothed over. Corn grows on the chalk, where chemical fertilizers make the ground productive, and modern short-stemmed varieties can stand up to the downland winds.

Like a drunkard making fixedly for the door, the Cuckmere wanders with a wavery elegance towards the sea. The gradient is almost nil; there is scarcely any invitation for the river to arrive at its mouth. It has been here for a long time and is certainly older than the chalk Downs that surround it. As the hills rose about forty million years ago, an outer ripple of the Alpine cataclysm far to the south, the river maintained its erosive course. Now it lolls easily in the old and comfortable bed it has made for itself. But there is change implicit in the scene. If this were not a still but a film taken over thousands of years, one frame a century, you would see the meanders of the river moving to and fro across the valley over time, as slipperily mobile as an eel wriggling in the bed of its home.

overleaf

BOSHAM HARBOUR
West Sussex

Perhaps this is too strong a historical vision of the landscape, but one could see this little yacht, tied up on the salty shores of Bosham harbour in south Sussex, as floating in the waters of melted glaciers. This is a drowned river valley, created when the world warmed up about ten thousand years ago, when England was cut from the continent of Europe. This deeply land-locked harbour is one of several along this coast, where Sussex extends a muddy many-fingered hand into the sea. Bosham does not have the pert conclusiveness of a Cornish fishing village, neatly whitewashed within the nick of a rocky shore. But there is something more alluring than that, less obvious, about these soft, lowland English harbours, half-worlds where the margin is uncertain between one element and another, where the tide seeps in and out of the spongy marshes and where, big, plain-faced Georgian brick houses look out across the mud. This is said to be the place where Canute failed to command the sea. His daughter is buried in the church.

NEAR ABBOTSBURY
Dorset

The first leaves of spring stipple the dry sticks of a thorn hedge. This is open, champaign country, the westernmost chalk in England, before the rock changes underfoot and the country plunges into the tightly knit bocage of west Dorset and Devon. A slight hint of big country farming appears in the tramlines made by the chemical-spreading tractor as it drove up and down the field. The barn itself is built of the honey-coloured oolitic limestone from just to the west of here and roofed with reeds from the shallows of the Fleet, the long brackish lagoon dammed by the shingle of Chesil Bank. It marks the transition to a different kind of country.

————

LYME REGIS
Dorset

From the pale height of Golden Cap in the distance, Lyme Bay swings around in a calm, easy curve eaten out of soft rocks. It moves on past the clammy grey of the marls in which the bones of the first dinosaurs in England were discovered and where grimy half-troglodytic palaeonotologists are still to be seen, especially after heavy rain, digging through the ancient debris for stones and fossils. Past the small dip of Charmouth, you come to the huge, slimy dark landslip of the Black Ven and arrive at the ice-cream sweetness of Lyme Regis. It is, at least in part, a deliberate effect. The strawberry-flavoured row on the front, Madeira Cottages, were built with self-conscious prettiness in mind in the 1840s.

———

WISTMAN'S WOOD
Dartmoor, Devon

A survey of Dartmoor made in the very first years of the seventeenth century stumbled across 'some acres of wood and trees, that are a fathom about, and yet no taller than a man may touch to top with his hand, which is called Wistman's Wood.' It's a Tolkein place, unshaped and primitive, gnarled by the western weather and with the granite clitters, by which the oak seedlings are first protected, clothed in a skin of moss and lichen. Wistman was never a man; the name probably comes from the now-forgotten word *wisht*; it means haunted, the spooked place.

A MAYTIME HEDGE
The Lizard, Cornwall

On the southernmost point of England at the height of its spring, the stone walls, especially on the eastern side where they are sheltered from the all-pervasive westerlies coming in off the Atlantic, burst into flower as almost nowhere else in the country. This is the background to a medieval tapestry: the thrift in all its varieties and densities of pink, the bird's foot trefoil and the foxglove spears, the one or two white garlic bells at the foot of the hedge and the as yet unopened spikes of pennywort that crown it. The gorse not yet out is the only reminder that this is not a garden display, but the flowering on the edge of an acid moorland, the Goonhilly Downs.

CADGWITH
Cornwall

In this village on the Lizard television actors and media stars have their holiday cottages. It is hedged around with National Trust land and you might think that Cadgwith has become too cosy for its own good. But there is one thing that does something to preserve it: there is no harbour and it can never be a yachtie's favourite. The fishing boats, almost all of which are now catching shellfish, have to be pulled up by the motor winch housed in the building that gives on to the beach. The timber baulks over which the boats get hauled are left casually around, the sign says 'Keep clear of chains and blocks' – not holiday things – and with some relief you recognize a place where fudge is not the only issue.

———

KYNANCE COVE
Cornwall

The truth about Kynance has been known for many decades. 'During the season,' a guidebook writer remarked in 1910, 'it is like a corner of a fashionable watering place, covered with tourists, refreshment booths and sellers of serpentine.' These have been tidied away a little by the National Trust which now owns the cove. 'But autumn and winter bring a grand solitude when all traces of the trippers are washed away: the storms cleanse it with their mighty visitations. Only the white sands, the black and richly stained rocks remain, a haunt of homeless winds and crying gulls.' A. L. Salmon, the author of this, ended on a practical note. It is not a place, he said, 'where father and mother can recline restfully without constant anxiety for their boys and girls.' No, it is not. In a winter storm Kynance terrifies.

POLDHU COVE
Cornwall

Poldhu means the black harbour, but that is a side which strangers, non-fishermen, will never see. Instead, these inviting swathes of colour, the plateful of blue sea, the billowing pinks, the splash of sand, the distant cliffside turf: the coloured dream of England turning towards Gauguin. It is beautiful, at least in part, because it is so unexpected. Colour, full unabashed colour like this, is somehow not entirely English. Such a frank expression of the beautiful, and on such a scale, hardly seems to belong to a country whose national food is little more than porridge and prunes.

previous page

LOE BAR
AND LOE POOL
Porthleven, Cornwall

The Loe Bar, a bank of sand carried along the shore by the winds and currents, blocks the outlet of the River Caber that comes down to the coast from Helston. The blocked river valley is now the Loe Pool, two miles of still water fringed with dank woodland. The river was shut off in the thirteenth century, killing Helston as a port, but in the Victorian Arthur boom, the Loe Bar came to be seen as the place where after the last great battle, in Tennyson's version, Sir Bedivere carried the wounded Arthur.

And bore him to a chapel nigh the field,
A broken chancel with a broken cross,
That stood on a dark strait of barren land.
On one side lay the Ocean, and on one
Lay a great water, and the moon was full.

In the reedy fringes of the Loe Pool, according to this impossible vision, Bedivere twice hid the beautiful sword before finally obeying his king and casting it into the waters of the lake.

ST ENODOC CHURCH
near Rock, Cornwall

The distant tower on Stepper Point marks the mouth of the Camel Estuary, where the windsurfers play in the breeze coming in off the Bristol Channel. The little church of St Enodoc, with its small bent spire, sits half-buried in the dunes that surround it. For hundreds of years, at least from the end of the sixteenth century, the church – known as 'Sinking Neddy' – was almost entirely covered by the encroaching sand. But to collect his tithes the vicar had to ensure that services were still held there at least once a year and he, his acolytes, the marrying couples and their congregations all had to climb in and out through a hole in the roof. The church was unearthed in about 1870 and this churchyard, with its fringe of tamarisk trees, was the place where John Betjeman chose to be buried.

PORLOCK WEIR
near Minehead, Somerset

The Bristol Channel, with its ferocious forty-foot tides and the lack of any very good harbour between Land's End and Bristol, has always been one of the most dangerous seas around the English coast. Porlock Weir, where the wooded heights of the eastern edge of Exmoor stretch up from the harbour, is typical of the little gaps in the coastline where small boats can run for shelter when the weather turns bad. There was an attempt in the nineteenth century to turn it into a mineral port, shipping lead ore from here to the industrial centres in south Wales, but the enterprise was never viable and the place remains now small, marginal and obscure.

GLASTONBURY TOR
Somerset

From the banks of the River Brue, canal-ized as it crosses the wet flatlands of the Somerset Levels, the isolated hill of Glastonbury Tor, crowned by the tower of the ruined St Michael's Church, stands as an island from an earlier sea. Legend has gathered around Glastonbury: it is now one of the headquarters of ley-line seekers and astrological visionaries, and said by many to be one of the mouths of hell. But Glastonbury was not always as eccentric as it has now become. It was certainly one of the earliest Christian sites in England, was the richest abbey in the country, outdoing even Fountains in Yorkshire, and was believed in the Middle Ages to be the place where Joseph of Arimathaea's staff grew into a winter-flowering thorn. The tree was cut down by a mad Puritan (he was blinded by chips flying from the stump) but some of its descendants are still growing there. Botanists have analysed them and found the thorn to be an otherwise unknown variety whose nearest relatives grow in Syria.

CLIFTON SUSPENSION BRIDGE
and River Avon, Bristol

Clifton Suspension Bridge, designed by Brunel in 1829, was not actually completed until thirty-five years later, when Brunel himself was long dead. But the great engineer's conception remained clear throughout. 'A work of art thus thrown across such grand and imposing scenery,' he wrote, 'should be as simple and unobtrusive as possible, that it should fix the observer rather by the grandeur of the ideas that it gave rise to than attract his attention by anything inconsistent with the surrounding objects.' If only the designers of the 1960s flats, the jerky little footbridge and the polychrome 1980s apartments with their pantiled roofs had had Brunel's words singed into their brains.

overleaf

ROYAL CRESCENT
Bath, Avon

This oval piazza sliced in half and exposed to a spread of lawn (earlier pictures show cows grazing in front of it) represents what, in a wish-fulfilment world, the model English capital would have looked like. The plan and design made by John Wood the Younger in 1767 makes a single palace of a street of thirty houses. It is perhaps characteristic of the English that although the Crescent looks like a single imperial development, many of the houses were built as speculative investments by small groups of local builders and craftsmen. As you can tell from the party-walls dividing the roof line, they vary in width from three to four bays and behind this uniform façade are widely different in plan. When the Crescent was finished, a guidebook to Bath could say that the city had now been so transformed 'as to be able to vie with any city in Europe in the politeness of its amusements and the elegance of its accommodations . . .'

A weed, it is said, is an attitude of mind and this picture, which might be ordinary enough in Spain or Switzerland, has come to seem almost miraculous in the south of England. The Wylye valley in Wiltshire is now smart and expensive country, where straw pheasants and even trout now strut and leap along the ridges of newly thatched houses. There is not much sign now of the sort of life recorded by W. H. Hudson in 1910 when he claimed that the ladies of the villages in this valley grew yellow stonecrop around the doors of their cottages because it went by the local name of Welcome-home-husband-though-never-so-drunk. Closer to the modern world was Robert Byron. This part of Wiltshire was, he wrote in 1935, 'a new discovery, a beauty spot fragrant to the soul, which fulfils the twin conditions of such a title: convenient access from London, and an appearance of reposeful good taste unblemished by mountains, cliffs, moors, or any other dramatic natural features.'

overleaf

STONEHENGE
Wiltshire

The first structures here were built around 2200 BC. Stonehenge continued in use, not as an isolated object but as part of a heavily-used landscape, filled with houses, farms and workshops, until about 1240 BC – a thousand years, almost exactly the age of our oldest cathedrals.

The temple becomes itself around dawn, the moment, in Thomas Hardy's beautiful phrase at the end of *Tess of the d'Urbervilles*, when 'the whole enormous landscape bore that impress of reserve, taciturnity and hesitation which is usual just before day . . .' Certainly the huge chthonic presence of the stones themselves are what one remembers, but there is more to it than that. This is obviously a sky temple, hinged to the light and the space around it, placed only casually and deftly on the plain, not in a geographical climax but in a slight and subtle billow of the chalk.

BOWOOD HOUSE
Wiltshire

In the distance Charles Barry's Victorian tower dominates the portico and colonnades of Robert Adam's Diocletian wing of Bowood House built in the 1760s. That is all that remains of a much larger building; most of it was demolished in 1955 by the Marquis of Lansdowne. (Its dining room was carefully dismantled and is now to be found enshrined as a boardroom in Richard Rogers's Lloyds building in the City.) At least Capability Brown's park and lake – together they cover 1,000 acres – remain relatively complete. The gentle serenity of Brown's style is still there, its optimistic and seducing calm. He was first summoned to inspect the place's 'capabilities' in 1761 during his first boom period (his fee at the time was ten guineas a day), when creating huge acreages of aesthetic landscape at Chatsworth, Alnwick, Syon, Blenheim and Richmond among many others. This, like the others, was designed as a picture of an expensive Eden.

St Andrew's Church was restored by the Rudge family in the 1730s and at that time given its characteristically eighteenth-century medievalist look. Those little battlements are the badge of an age. It now appears in the park at Wheatfield as little more than an eye-catcher, a visual incident in an aesthetic ensemble. There should be a house here too, but it burnt down in 1814 and all that is left is this charming fragment. The removal of the house does something interesting to the seigneurial landscape; it takes away the element of *power*. Wheatfield would never have been as grand as the landscape at Bowood, but to compare the two as they now are is intriguing. The house makes the park at Bowood worldy; Wheatfield is an innocent.

————

LOWER SLAUGHTER
Gloucestershire

Why is it that the Cotswold village is the touchstone of picture-England? Perhaps because nothing is discordant there, because incongruity has for decades been seen as a sort of visual crime in the Cotswolds. The colours and textures of the stone tile roofs and of the rubblestone walls of the houses, the gardens and even (a twentieth-century addition) the banks of the river all fold in quite comfortably with each other. The mostly seventeenth-century architecture – real or repro – is strict in its verticals and horizontals. There is not a flounce to be seen. This is demure politeness turned to stone, as blank-eyed as a congregation during the sermon, as un-troubled as a couple retired to their armchairs. It's England in cardigans.

NAUNTON
Gloucestershire

Jonathan Raban once said that he was unable to live in the English countryside because he was no good at 'the strenuous moral art of villaging'. And doesn't a village like Naunton in the Windrush valley look like a diagram of the social tensions, alliances and internal fine distinctions that characterize real life in a village? Near the church at the west end (its big square-headed windows are from an Elizabethan rebuild) the smart, older houses, with fine, fluffy trees clumped over them, gather together in what must be the socially-superior end. But straggling out eastwards, taking in the Baptist chapel (1850) and the school (1864), you come to the picture windows, immature gardens and modern Cotswold-style additions which mark-out non-establishment Naunton. It would not take a detective to guess what the relationship between these two parts of Naunton might be.

In 1973 Britain joined the Common Market and became eligible for the Common Agricultural Policy subsidy on oil seed rape. The farmers took it up in a big way. Less than 43,000 acres of rape had been planted in 1972; more than 1.1 million acres were covered with it by the spring of 1992. Rape has changed the look and, at the flowery stage, the smell of England.

The country and the Common Market as a whole is now very nearly self-sufficient in the oil and it is unlikely that many more acres will be given over to rape in the future. Do people mind about it? Perhaps only the profoundly conservative and the beekeepers who say their honey has been coarsened. And if the subsidy is withdrawn and Europe is happy enough to import its rape seed oil again from the Third World, can't you hear the old boys in 2042 reminiscing over those wonderful yellow fields of their youth, the splash of sunshine enlivening England's ubiquitous green?

STANWAY HOUSE
Gloucestershire

Here is an English yellow, the sunniest, treacliest colour that English stone can ever be. And the Caroline architecture (about 1630) of the famous gateway into Stanway matches the flamboyance of the stone. The cockle shells that decorate it front and back and sides (as they do the other gateway glimpsed through the arch) are the badge of the Tracy family (motto: The Tracys, the Tracys, the wind in their face is) who at the Dissolution took over Stanway from Tewkesbury Abbey, to which it had belonged for the previous 600 years.

The church of St Peter was savagely scraped in 1896 when the Tracy family pew was also removed. The pew was actually glassed in and on one occasion in the early nineteenth century a particularly ferocious châtelaine, hearing that the vicar was about to preach on the need for a Sunday school for the village children, said 'I will not have the village educated,' very loudly, shut the window of the pew and did not open it until he had returned to a less subversive form of worship.

GLOUCESTER DOCKS
and Cathedral

The huge mid-fifteenth century tower of Gloucester Cathedral climbs above the roof of the old office of the Gloucester and Berkeley Canal Company. The canal, running south-west from here to Sharpness, cut out the bends and shifting mudbanks of the Severn. When it was finished in 1827, this was the largest ship canal in the world. Gloucester dock was the entrepôt, where all the goods from the industrial Midlands, which had arrived here on older and narrower canals, were transferred to the sea-going ships that had made their way up from the Bristol Channel. This, like almost every non-containerized port in the world, has now been restored, cleaned and sweetened. The giant warehouses contain the National Waterways Museum and the quasi-medieval vessel moored on the left is a Danish trawler rebuilt for a film about Christopher Columbus.

overleaf

NEAR CINDERFORD
Gloucestershire

The best places are always the unpreserved, the undeclared, the uncorrected and the undisturbed. That this is a Norman fortified place on the far side of the River Severn and that the beech trees are a gentlemanly planting from the last century is good because both go so unremarked. Like the presence of meaning at Little Gidding, it is far better for not being laid out on a plate. Littledean allows itself to come stealing up on you unannounced. Nothing is worse than the harsh restoration or the boring notice.

————

LOWER BROCKHAMPTON
Hereford and Worcester

Every farm along the Welsh borders is carved out of what was once a vast and continuous oak forest. Lower Brockhampton was made in about 1380 of the trees that surrounded it. The moat, which like many is only three-sided, and the charming, indefensible fifteenth-century gatehouse, are there as status symbols, gestures towards the grand by a family of yeoman farmers, the Domultons. The gatehouse, with its close-studded timbers and its upper storey jettied out on all four sides (an urban and so fashionable habit), was probably built a century later than the cheaper, square-panelled construction of most of the main house. These half-timbered buildings are the origins of bypass architecture, perhaps because they could be imitated so cheaply. Even these originals were pre-fabs and extremely efficient use of time and material. The wooden skeletons were prepared away from site in a 'framyngplace', probably in the winter, and then carried here for erection in the spring.

NEAR KINGTON
Hereford and Worcester

Even if sometimes it is tempting to think of England as hedged and walled, 'a honeycomb of particularities', as Ronald Blythe has called it, there is something else, particularly out on the western edges, where the long, loping rhythms of the country reaching out towards Wales are an invitation in themselves. The unrestrictedness of this is English too, that drawing of the eye to the horizon, in which landscape after landscape is folded away – what is this but a picture of walking country?

The Bakewell to Buxton railway, opened in 1863, slices across the valley of the Derbyshire Wye as it curves round from Upperdale to Monsal Dale. John Ruskin had loved this place before the railway came. 'You might have seen the gods there,' he exaggerated, 'morning and evening, walking in fair procession on the lawns, and to and fro among the pinnacles of its crags, but the valley is gone and the gods with it, and now every fool in Buxton can be at Bakewell in half an hour and every fool in Bakewell at Buxton; which you might think a lucrative process of exchange . . .' Gods for money: not a favourite Victorian deal. But people are adaptable. When British Rail closed the line and proposed to demolish the viaduct there was an outcry. It was given a preservation order in 1970.

overleaf

Limestone: riddled with caves and secret watercourses, where streams disappear underground into fern-lined holes; where the exposed stone is cut into miniature clefts and nodules like a fossilized and fragmentary map of the brain; where the turf is carpeted with thyme and sprinkled with scabious; where black and ochre stains colour the white cliffs in enormous abstracts. Why is this the most bewitching of all rocks? W. H. Auden provided the best answer: 'If it form the one landscape that we, the inconstant ones, are consistently homesick for, this is chiefly because it dissolves in water.' Here at Malham Cove a water-rotted cliff confronts the net of field and wall in Airedale, a piece of dissolving upland facing the valley below it.

MIDDLESMOOR
Nidderdale,
North Yorkshire

The level brow of the high Pennines closes off the far end of Nidderdale, a dead-end valley where Middlesmoor, as the last village in the gritstone dale, sits high on its ridge to catch the first of the morning light.

This valley has become a battleground of environmentalist politics. As long ago as 1947, in the Hobhouse Report, Nidderdale was recommended as one of the new Areas of Outstanding Natural Beauty. Local objections, both from the farmers, who do not like the idea of restrictions on their farming practices, and from people who live in the dale, who fear the increase in tourism, meant that by 1992 nothing had happened. The new status would mean increased government grants, but also increased planning controls (no satellite dishes and no house extensions). Is this an example of a pastoral vision being imposed on local people, the twentieth-century equivalent of eighteenth-century villagers being housed in *cottages ornées* because only they were acceptable in the view?

RICHMOND
North Yorkshire

The shops and pubs that line the cobbled marketplace in Richmond mark what was once the wall of the outer bailey of the castle, from whose tower this photograph was taken. This is the châtelain's view, the burghers gathered at his feet like a provincial court. Holy Trinity sits in the middle of the marketplace as one of the strangest buildings in the country. The church itself is on the first floor, until recently there were shops beneath it and that shopping centre-cum-nave is joined to the tower by a small office block. But more important than any of these eccentricities is the style of Richmond, a town looking like a tweed suit, a farmer at a christening, shined shoes, ruddy face, a sort of highly textured straightness. There is nowhere quite like it in the country.

SWALEDALE
*near Low Row,
North Yorkshire*

Look at the walls in this picture. This is what went into them: good scarcement (the buried footings); throughbands at 21 inches to bind the faces of the wall together; well-fitted hearting in the core of the wall but without any earth in it which might retain the water and burst the wall when the frosts came; a coverband at 40 inches; and then a good copestone, set vertical or leaning a little uphill, to bring the wall up to 4 feet 6 inches, solid and almost indestructible. A man could do 6 or 7 yards a day and it is this that has made the landscape, or at least its skeleton. And it creates a picture of visual certainty, of the well-ordained life, neither cramped nor isolated, neither uncomfortable nor lush, in which there is order but an order imposed with a sensitivity to the local quirks and vagaries. It is an order without rigidity.

Yewbarrow on the left, Great Gable at the far end, Lingmell to the right of it and the slopes of Scafell Pike disappearing up into the cloud: this is England as Norway, the glacial valley, the vastly deepened lake, the slithery screes, the top end of England, the country of the national sublime. That idea only appears at a certain moment in our history – the Wordsworth moment – and the unresponsive and the narrow-minded continue to poo-poo it. Auden provided the best riposte to them all:

> *Am I*
> *To see in the Lake District, then,*
> *Another bourgeois invention like the piano?*

he asked, and then quite blankly answered his own question:

> *Well, I won't.*
> *overleaf*

WASDALE HEAD
Cumbria

When you are up on the side of Kirk Fell looking out at the blade of flatland surrounded by the highest hills in the country, you can forget all the history of the place, the legislation that keeps it looking as though nothing really has ever happened here. Wasdale at different times has been threatened with blanket spruce forest and with a scheme to use the lake as a reservoir for the nuclear plant at Sellafield. The National Trust saved it all and Wasdale Head will always be, in the minds of those who are open to it, a wild and poetic place. Will Ritson, the landlord of the Wasdale Head Inn, the white-faced building at the foot of the dark bulk of Yewbarrow, used to tell the story of an eagle he found on the fellside one winter evening, lying there with a broken wing. He took it to his yard and while the wing was mending kept the eagle in the chicken run. One night a foxhound bitch got into the run. Ritson was worried for the eagle but it seemed to have survived undamaged. Five months later the bitch gave birth to a litter of winged hounds.

RIVER DERWENT
at Grange-in-Borrowdale, Cumbria

A layered landscape: ten thousand years ago this valley was filled to the brim with glacier ice. Up on the crags of the beautifully named High Spy in the background every rock shows the signs of its own abrasion. On the right hand side the ridge is made of the soft and smoothable Skiddaw slates; in the middle and on the left are the hard, dark, shaggy Borrowdale Volcanics. The glacier left them knobbled. In the valley it is a Viking landscape (Borrowdale means the valley of the fortress in Old Norse) where tiny hamlets are scattered among the garden-sized fields. During the Middle Ages Borrowdale belonged to Furness Abbey (Grange means monastic farm). The monks used it as a cattle ranch. After the Dissolution, small independent men – called Statesmen in the Lake District – built stone farmhouses like the one glimpsed here at the far end of the bridge. Wordsworth thought painting them white ruined a landscape.

In trailed, stony skirts the old slate quarries at Tilberthwaite dump the waste below them. These quarries are now almost entirely defunct and are used for rock-climbing, sub-aqua diving (in the rain-water pools that have filled the excavations) and parties so wild the police have put a stop to them. New permissions to quarry in the National Park continue to be given, partly to provide local jobs and partly so that new buildings can have roofs that do not look hideous in the Lake District towns and villages. But can that be right? Keswick and Kendal are ugly anyway. What can be the point of blasting away another Cumbrian hill in an attempt to beautify the irredeemable?

In the far distance, beyond Watendlath Fell, the west wind blows its banner of cloud away from the summit of Ullscarf. Does this look like England? This is the Tyrol isn't it? It is worth considering that the version of Romanticism now associated with the Lake District was simply an influx into English culture of a foreign and essentially European way of seeing things. Coleridge in particular was profoundly moulded by German idealist philosophy. The only part of England that could fit this European vision was its most continental and un-English of landscapes, the *alpen* of Watendlath and Borrowdale. *Lyrical Bal-* *lads* was written in the Quantocks but no one ever talks about the school of 'Somerset Poets' precisely because Somerset could never have provided the right picture.

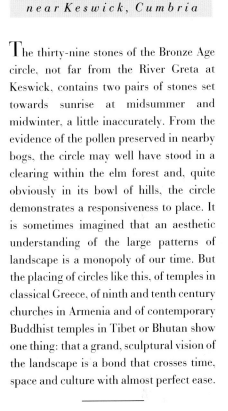

The thirty-nine stones of the Bronze Age circle, not far from the River Greta at Keswick, contains two pairs of stones set towards sunrise at midsummer and midwinter, a little inaccurately. From the evidence of the pollen preserved in nearby bogs, the circle may well have stood in a clearing within the elm forest and, quite obviously in its bowl of hills, the circle demonstrates a responsiveness to place. It is sometimes imagined that an aesthetic understanding of the large patterns of landscape is a monopoly of our time. But the placing of circles like this, of temples in classical Greece, of ninth and tenth century churches in Armenia and of contemporary Buddhist temples in Tibet or Bhutan show one thing: that a grand, sculptural vision of the landscape is a bond that crosses time, space and culture with almost perfect ease.

———————

NORTH ROW
Cambo, Northumberland

The village where Capability Brown was born in 1716 does everything now of which Brown would have disapproved. Sweet peas, honeysuckle and roses are trained as nature would never have had them: these are unclassical, unsymmetrical and un-smart things. Cambo was remodelled in the 1740s by Sir Walter Calverley Blackett, the owner of 13,000 acres of the surrounding county, a local politician rich from coal and other mercantile interests in Newcastle. There was a village here before but he regularized it into three parallel streets, Front, Middle and North Rows. Blackett's heirs gave the whole estate to the National Trust during the war and most of these cottages are now lived in by NT staff.

HARTHOPE BURN
The Cheviots,
Northumberland

Yellow balsam grows in the stream and nettles among the granite boulders on the bank. At the eastern end of the Scottish border, the huge lumpen mass of the Cheviots creates a satisfactory boundary between the countries, a barren, empty upland, beyond which the accents change and the loyalties alter. This is reiving, raiding country where until the Act of Union in 1703 the rich lived in pocket fortresses and the poor in houses so lightly constructed that they could be dismantled at the news of an approaching Scottish raid and so escape a burning. As Vanbrugh said of Northumberland: 'There is nothing here of the tame, sneaking south.'

BAMBURGH CASTLE
Northumberland

Bamburgh Castle on the North Sea coast stands 150 feet above the sand on the last outcrop of the Whin Sill, a band of hard volcanic dolerite that stutters out to sea beyond Bamburgh as the Farne Islands. In 547 Ida the Flamebearer, King of Northumbria, (why do we not have names like that any more?) built the first castle here and the rock has remained continuously inhabited ever since. The Kings of Northumbria and Bernicia were crowned here, it was wrecked by Vikings, restored by Henry I, and now belongs to the Armstrongs, the arms' manufacturers from Newcastle, and is divided into flats.

———————

CITY OF DURHAM

Durham mirrors Bath as alternative visions of a capital city: northern, medieval and feudal against southern, enlightened and bourgeois. This was the capital of the Bishops Palatine of Durham, a semi-independent fief anchored to the twin mass of the Norman cathedral and the castle crouched next to it. The Prince Bishops were able to create their own knights and barons of the palatinate, raise money and armies, and try cases both civil and criminal. Only in 1836 were Durham's rights surrendered to the Crown. Nowhere else in the country is the joint lay and temporal power so starkly compacted. And in that Durham seems unEnglish. Wouldn't it feel more at home in Germany?

———

HIGH FORCE
Teesdale, County Durham

The peat-thick whisky of the Tees crashes over a lip of dolerite (it is the same volcanic rock as the lump on which Bamburgh Castle is built) into the softer limestone of Teesdale that surrounds it. The dolerite, which was squeezed into the limestone as a lava, stiffens into a brittle rock. It chips and fragments along the fault lines inside it, the cracks which appeared as the lava cooled underground. There are no soft edges here but as consolation you can just make out in the nicks and crevices the small relieving points of forget-me-not blue and harebell purple.

previous page

The River Esk eases out to the North Sea between the high banks on which Whitby is built. This is the only haven for ships of any size in a hundred mile stretch of coast between the Humber and the Tees. It is a place hinged to the sea, made almost exclusively of brick and pantiles, both of which arrived here by ship, one as ballast, the other as cargo. On the skyline is the ruined abbey, shelled by the Germans in the First World War, and below it to the left the seamen's church of St. Mary.

Whitby was once the great shipbuilding centre of the north-east. In the Whitehall Yard in the foreground, now defunct, the *Discovery*, one of the ships of Captain Cook's last voyage to the Pacific, was built in 1774. There are plans afoot to turn the yard into a Captain Cook theme park, complete with a full-scale floating replica of the *Endeavour*.

NORTH YORK MOORS
near Rosedale,
North Yorkshire

Heather coats the big, smooth upland of the North York Moors. Below them in detail the Dales remain a Danish landscape. These dispersed farms, equally distributed among the valley fields, repeat a pattern still to be found in the country from which the first settlers came. It is always the pattern that survives, rather than the fabric, and if you blind your eyes to the neat seventeenth- and eighteenth-century farmhouses, you can be sure that you are looking at a pattern of field, hedge, lane and settlement not very different from a sunny day in the Dark Ages.

SPAUNTON MOOR
near Rosedale Abbey,
North Yorkshire

People often say that moorland is nothing better than a wet desert. And those people often represent the forestry interests who have coated so much English moorland with their hideous trees. But you only have to see this desert in bloom to realize what a sin those vast, square-edged conifer plantations have been. This moor, like so many, is managed for grouse by occasionally setting fire to it. It may well be this alone that prevents the moors from being taken over by a sort of small and scrubby woodland. That would be a loss. Never again would you have this wonderful open width and the long, long horizons.

CASTLE HOWARD
North Yorkshire

Perhaps English baroque is a contradiction in terms. Certainly this garden front of Castle Howard, begun by Vanbrugh and Hawksmoor in 1700, would scarcely qualify as baroque on the continent of Europe. But in scale alone the great Yorkshire palace steps outside the bounds of English *politesse*: 292 feet from wing to wing set in a vast decorative landscape, 'the noblest lawn in the world,' as Horace Walpole described it, 'fenced by half the horizon.' The Victorian Atlas Fountain, by John Thomas, Prince Albert's favoured sculptor, in which muscled tritons in twisted attitudes trumpet their conches, conforms more richly to the baroque idea.

NORMANTON
Leicestershire

In 1975 the little River Gwash in Rutland was dammed and 3,500 acres of its valley was drowned. A country house – Normanton Park – seven farms and sixteen cottages disappeared under the new reservoir. The church of St Matthew at Normanton was just on the edge and was saved, in Nikolaus Pevsner's words, 'stripped of its dignity, up to its knees in concrete and rubble on an artificial spit jutting out into Rutland Water'. The church was not a particularly distinguished building, the work of two London architects, the tower made in the 1820s, the rest in 1911. So was this the right thing to have done? Perhaps not. It looks unnatural, too much of a compromise. No landscape designer would ever have chosen to have done this if he had been given a free hand. Normanton would have been better off utterly drowned. Or perhaps they should have lowered the dam by a foot or two and then the lake waters would have lapped calmly at St Matthew's west door.

previous page

TRIANGULAR LODGE
Rushton,
Northamptonshire

If there is such a thing as coherent madness, this is surely it: a three storey, three-sided building, of which each side is thirty-three and one third feet long, decorated with three windows on each floor of each side, each with three triangular gables, with three mottoes, each of thirty-three letters, (QVIS SEPARABIT NOS A CHARITATE CHRISTI— Who will take us from the love of Christ?) and marked with the date 1593, itself divisible by three to the power of three, the year in which the lodge was designed. It is nothing but a profession of faith – the Trinity turned into stone – and a pun on its author's name. Sir Thomas Tresham was converted to Catholicism in 1580 and spent fifteen of the next twenty-five years under arrest for his faith. The Triangular Lodge could only have been built at one particular moment in English history. The Middle Ages could have produced nothing so abstracted; a hundred years later, it would have become a classical temple.

In 1625 Nicholas Ferrar, a Cambridge don, who had travelled throughout Europe, found himself suddenly rich on the death of his father. He bought the estate at Little Gidding, near Huntingdon, 'which place he

chose,' according to Izaak Walton, 'for the privacy of it, and for the Hall, which had the parish church or chapel belonging and adjoining near to it; for Mr. Ferrar having seen the manners and vanities of the world, and found them to be, as Mr. Herbert says, a nothing between two dishes, did so contemn it, that he resolved to spend the remainder of his life in mortifications, and in devotion and charity, and to be always prepared for death . . .' Ferrar and his family and about thirty others lived the life of a small monastic community here. Ferrar died in 1639 and is buried in front of the chapel. The community, which Charles I had visited at least once, was eventually broken up by Parliamentary troops. Eliot visited Little Gidding in 1936 and wrote the poem of the same name five years later.

———

BARN HILL
Stamford, Lincolnshire

The best English streets are beautiful for their disorganization. This is not the Piazza del Popolo: neighbours are neglected, the buildings are not consistent in their style, material, the line they make with the street or in the heights of their roofs. Everything is done exclusively for itself. It is at least sewn together by the beautiful stone from the nearby Ketton and Barnack quarries and by the stone slates from Collyweston a few miles to the west. Reading up the right-hand side of the street, No. 3 has a mid-eighteenth-century Chinese fret porch, No. 4 a strict early eighteenth-century front on an older house, and No. 6 a seventeenth-century bay with Georgian Gothick lights in the windows. On the left-hand side closest to us, No. 12 has a late seventeenth-century double-curved pediment on richly carved brackets. No. 13 beyond it, with surrounds to the windows in the manner of James Gibbs, was built in 1740, as chic as a small Tuscan palazzo. The miracle is the absence of cars.

NEAR SPALDING
Lincolnshire

In the light silt soil of south Lincolnshire, where the water table is high and the drainage almost perfect, tulips have been grown since the 1930s. Unemployed Dutchmen came over during the slump and brought with them both bulbs and expertise to found the English tulip business. It peaked in the 1950s when 6,000 acres around Spalding were devoted to bulbs. Most of the growing has now returned to Holland (Spalding families have specialized in daffodils) and only 300 acres of tulips are now planted each year in Lincolnshire. This extraordinary scene does not last more than a day or two. The bulb suffers if the flower is allowed to last too long. The day after this picture was taken, the farmer moved through his tulips, decapitating every one.

———

HOLKHAM HALL
Norfolk

The Earl of Leicester, possessor of 44,000 acres of prime Norfolk, commissioned the masterpiece of Holkham from William Kent in 1734. The almost unapproachable severity of this Roman house (beside it Castle Howard begins to look flouncy) is set within the easy perfections of a William Kent landscape. As Horace Walpole remarked, Kent 'felt the delicious contrast of hill and valley turning into each other, tasted the beauty of the gentle swell, or concave scoop, and remarked how loose groves crowned an easy eminence with happy ornament.' House and landscape need each other, the mutually enhancing presence in the landscape of the masculine and the feminine.

previous page

WELLS-NEXT-THE-SEA
Norfolk

'Currents' No. 29, 'Happy Days' No. 30: the English seaside hut totters on around the bay, the gentle and the slightly private, the half-heard conversations through the match-thin wooden walls, the world of rugs and thermoses and sand inside the pants, the buried dog mess, the persistent wasp, the Ribena spilt over the floor, the teenage flirting with four huts down, the wrap-around cardigans and plastic shoes, the winter abandonment, the last look out to sea, the return next early summer to an unforgotten smell – scrubbed boards, cobwebs and the stagnant pool of locked-in air.

CLEY·NEXT·THE·SEA
Norfolk

Cley behind the parapet of its sea-defences, which the Norfolk reeds in the marshes wash up to like a tide, is a fossil. This was once a seaport and a fishing village, but as more and more seabanks were built to take in more and more of the saltmarsh to turn it into pasture, the little River Glaven that runs out to sea here slowed up. Its channels were no longer scoured by the tides and eventually, in a sclerotic condition, Cley, as so many other places along the Norfolk coast, died as a commercial port. It now takes its place on a muffled coast, where these villages find themselves miles back from the sea. It is their great charm, their half-seaside nature. And this process has come full-circle: precisely because they can do no business nowadays they have remained pretty and so become expensive. Nowhere thrives like a fossil.

———

BLICKLING HALL
Norfolk

The yew hedges like creaky sofas continue the lovely curlicued and moustachioed gable ends of the entrance court at Blickling. For all its symmetry, there is a naivety, a show-off air in the appearance of this house, something which by the time of Holkham had been overlaid or left behind. It is the difference between a Jacobean portrait – the frame and posture quite stiff, the clothes immensely, even primitively decorated – and an eighteenth-century painting in which the people lounge in the landscape, where the clothes themselves have loosened and simplified, and where the long continuous surfaces of a single silk, with the buttons covered in the same material, take the place of the bobbled, jewelled, garnetted costumes their grandfathers wore.

———

ON THE
NORFOLK BROADS

Ever since the great Dutch paintings in the seventeenth century, the cow that stands in the water's edge or on the bank of a boggy pool has been a constant in pictures of a terrestrial Eden. What is it about cattle? Their placidity, their earthy, mottled colours? Perhaps, but the presence of these animals does something else: it introduces a *smell* to a picture, that sweet grass-into-milk smell, a sugary mousse of a smell, which a crowd of cattle always sends wafting across a field. That is why they are so good in a picture: they make it seem more real.

SOUTHWOLD
Suffolk

The 1890 lighthouse peers like an invigilator over Southwold's seaside roofs. None of them pay any attention. The buildings here are not particularly interesting in themselves (except perhaps for the seaside-eccentric bungalow at the corner — half-pink-half-whitewashed, half-Gothicky-half-picture-window — whose parts do not connect) but like the whole of this out-of-date town, stuck in 1953, this little seaside green works as the sort of place where it would obviously be nice to be. 'Nice' — the most used and most despised adjective in the language — is what the English want England to be. In Southwold they have got it.

previous page

WICKEN FEN
Cambridgeshire

Wicken Fen is an island of the past saved in the sea of the modern fenlands. Every year in the heavily exploited fields of Cambridgeshire and Lincolnshire the level of the pumped out peat drops another few inches. In some places the peat has gone entirely and the farmers are down to the nearly sterile clays beneath it. Wicken Fen is unique in that it literally stands proud of the land around it, a patch of unshrunken wetland, a large vegetable sponge which water has to be pumped *into*. It's a managed semi-wilderness, a pet piece of the slightly untidy in which the 700 species of moths and butterflies and the 200 different sorts of spider can all relax.

A careless shoe-string, in whose tie
I see a wild civility:
Do more bewitch me than when art
Is too precise in every part.

(Robert Herrick, *Delight in Disorder*, 1648)

HATFIELD FOREST
Essex

Pollards in a wood pasture (cut at this height so that the cows grazing beneath them would not be able to eat off the young shoots) create an utterly authentic picture of medieval and perhaps neolithic England. Certainly for 800 years and maybe for several thousand, Hatfield Forest has been managed in the same way, a careful interfolding of the demands of trees, deer, men and their cattle. It is a profoundly conservative place, the creation simply of slowness and almost endless repetition. All this remains there now, visitable, uniquely remarkable not as a piece of wilderness but of multiple symbiosis between man and the organisms on which he has relied, all within screaming distance of the end of the runway at Stansted Airport.

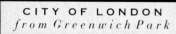

CITY OF LONDON
from Greenwich Park

London as it never is: a view. The eye swings round from the distant stub on the left of the NatWest Tower in the City, past the rectangles of 1960s tower blocks, the rehousing of a bombed East End, to the redevelopments of the Docklands in the middle distance, the tricksy flats and sleek-skinned offices, including the huge tower at Canary Wharf, and arrives in the foreground at Inigo Jones's Queen's House at Greenwich (1620), framed by the towers of Wren's Royal Naval College beyond it on the bank of the Thames.

ACKNOWLEDGEMENTS

The author, photographer and publishers would particularly like to thank Viscount Coke and the Trustees of the Holkham Estate, the Hon. Simon Howard, and Diana Lanham and the National Trust for all their help and for allowing us to photograph their properties: By courtesy of Viscount Coke and the Trustees of the Holkham Estate pp. 140–41; Hon. Simon Howard pp. 10–11, 128–9; The National Trust pp. 29, 86–7, 154–5.

The photographer would like to thank Debbie Prosser, Evelyn Meers, Tricia Passes, Rachel and Glenny Cutting, Tim Mason, Alison Ely and, in particular, his parents for their constant support and encouragement.

Both author and photographer would like to thank Alice Millington-Drake for her charm and efficiency.

Extract on p. 27: W. H. Auden, *In Time of War: XXVII*, by kind permission of Faber and Faber Ltd, *The English Auden: Poems, Essays and Dramatic Writings 1927–1939*, Edward Mendelson (ed.).

First published in 1992 by George Weidenfeld & Nicolson Ltd

This paperback edition first published in 1997 by Phoenix Illustrated
Orion Publishing Group, Orion House
5, Upper St. Martin's Lane
London WC2H 9EA

British Library Cataloguing-in-Publication Data
A catalogue record for this book is available from
the British Library

ISBN 1-85799-947-9

Edited by Alice Millington-Drake
Designed by Peter Bridgewater
Typeset at The Spartan Press Ltd., Lymington, Hants
Colour separations by Newsele Litho Ltd.
Printed and bound in Italy

Half-title page: Kirk Fell and Great Gable, Cumbria
Frontispiece: Cows, near Westonbirt, Gloucestershire
Pages 30-1: Lake Buttermere, Cumbria